R

Upadesa Saram

An interpretation by
Shirishkumar S. Murthy

'Purely by the grace of my Master, Ramesh Balsekar'

Other books by Shirishkumar S. Murthy

RAMANA MAHARSHI'S

Upadesa Saram

An interpretation by
Shirishkumar S. Murthy

'Purely by the grace of my Master, Ramesh Balsekar'

ZEN
PUBLICATIONS
A DIVISION OF MAOLI MEDIA PRIVATE LIMITED

Published by
ZEN PUBLICATIONS
A Division of Maoli Media Private Limited

60, Juhu Supreme Shopping Centre,
Gulmohar Cross Road No. 9, JVPD Scheme,
Juhu, Mumbai 400 049. India.
Tel: +91 22 32408074
eMail: info@zenpublications.com
Website: www.zenpublications.com

Credits
Cover & Book Design by Red Sky Designs, Mumbai

ISBN 13   978-81-88071-05-0

Printed by
Repro India Limited

Foreword

My Guru always said, 'Ramana Maharshi was my earliest inspiration. He still is.' I don't mind saying, 'Ramana Maharshi was my earliest "perspiration".' I came across *Maharshi's Gospel* twenty years ago and in spite of reading it a thousand times I felt that the core of Ramana Maharshi's teaching was eluding me. I began to understand the futility and the frustration in understanding the teaching intellectually.

Gradually, by the grace of Ramana Maharshi, I began yearning for His Presence. With great solicitude He guided me to Nisargadatta Maharaj who, in turn, guided me to my Guru, Ramesh S. Balsekar.

When I first met my Guru at His residence I was delighted to see Ramana Maharshi's photo prominently displayed in His study. Later on I was delighted to hear my Guru quote Maharshi with great affection and reverence. Within no time all my concepts dissolved.

My Guru, who is Ramana Maharshi in person for me, began explaining His concepts with great ease and perfection. I was so conditioned by Maharshi's concepts that God must have realized that I had to have a Guru who will initiate me into the path of Knowledge simplifying the words of Shri Ramana Maharshi.

After spending four months at my Guru's feet I began quoting freely from *Maharshi's Gospel* at the morning Satsangs. In one of the Satsangs I said, 'Ramana Maharshi says, surrender is a mighty prayer.' My Guru was delighted to hear it. He promptly asked me, 'From which book are you quoting?' I said, *Maharshi's Gospel,* and brought Him the book.

He read it with great affection and told me, 'Well, it was the destiny of this body-mind organism to come across this book now.' He then gave me *Upadesa Saram*. Strangely, I had never heard of this book. He told me to read *Upadesa Saram* every day.

I got totally absorbed by the book. It gave me the much needed insight that Ramana and Ramesh were one. By the grace of my Guru I began interpreting the *Upadesa Saram* and I am grateful to Him for accepting the first book which has happened through this body-mind organism.

Shirishkumar S. Murthy

Pointers from
Ramana Maharshi
❧

1.
Brahmacharya means living in Brahman, not celibacy.

2.
Constant *japa* repels all other thoughts.

3.
When *japa* becomes natural, it is realization.

4.
Vocal *japa* becomes mental, which is the same as meditation.

5.

The calm is greater than ecstasy and merges into *samadhi* leading to a 'waking sleep' state, always Consciousness.

6.

The ego-less 'I Am' is not a thought – it is realization.

7.

If the eyes are closed, it is *nirvikalpa*; if the eyes are open, it is *savikalpa*.

8.

The essence of the mind is awareness or Consciousness.

9.

The destruction of the mind is recognizing it as not being apart from the Self.

10.

The gap between two thoughts is the Self.

11.
There is no such thing as 'Realization' –
there is only the warding off of thoughts.

12.
Be fully conscious, be aware of people
and one's surroundings, without merging
in one's environment: retain an inner
independent awareness of THAT.

13.
A sharp, concentrated intellect is essential
in material matters but the revelation or
intuition arises in its own time.

14.
There is no thought of 'I' in true Being.

15.
If the ego is to go, something else must kill it.

16.
Ego disappears in sleep. It will be the
same in death.

17.
The ego is the 'I'-thought. The true 'I' is the SELF.

23.
Modern science admits that all matter is energy, Energy is SHAKTI. All is resolved into SHIVA-SHAKTI i.e. Self and mind.

24.
There is so much worry, so many Yoga techniques for such an obvious thing as 'Self-realization'!

25.
The Self, the Source, is a kind of sleepless sleep.

26.
Even a *jnani* looks forward to casting off his body.

27.
Sleep is temporary death. Death is longer sleep.

28.
There is no incarnation, either now or before or hereafter. This is the Truth.

29.
The Consciousness within, purged of the mind, is felt as God.

30.
That which 'IS' does not have to say 'I Am', for no thought arises that I am not!

31.
Both in the ignorant and the *jnani* the ego sprouts; but the *jnani's* ego is not dangerous: it is only the ash-skeleton of a burnt rope.

32.
Primarily, service to the Guru is to abide in the Self; but in practice it includes making his body comfortable in his abode.

33.
A man under sedation does not feel a slap, but that does not make him a *jnani*. *Jnana* is not inconsistent with the physical feeling of a slap.

34.
Education is learned ignorance.

35.
Silence between the Guru and the disciple is heart-to-heart speech.

36.
If the Guru believes that he can bestow realization by look or touch, he is not a real guru.

37.
The *jnani's* 'I' includes the body but without identification.

38.
The name Jehovah means 'I Am'.

39.
'Knowing' God means 'Being' God – it is not relative knowledge.

40.
To be 'still' is not to think.

– Ramesh S. Balsekar
15 September 1997

Knowledge blossoms into love.
Love blossoms into knowledge.

RAMESH BALSEKAR

❧❧❧

RAMANA MAHARSHI'S
Upadesa Saram
❦

कर्तुराज्ञया प्राप्यते फलम् ।
कर्म किं परं कर्म तज्जडम् ॥१॥

Karturaajnayaa praapyathe falam |
karma kim param karma tajjadam ॥

It is by the will of God that actions happen
followed by the fruits thereof. The sense of
doership is not superior. It is ineffective. Every
action is impersonal.

❧❧❧

कृति महोदधौ पतनकारणम् ।
फलमशाश्वतं गतिनिरोधकम् ॥२॥

Kriti mahodadhau pathankaaranam |
Falamashaashvatham gatinirodhakam ||

In the vast ocean of cause and effect, actions happen and impermanent results follow. If one takes them as 'my' action the idea of having a free will gets stronger. This sense of personal doership gives rise to the feeling of guilt or pride and effectively blocks the spiritual understanding that everything happens according to the will of God.

✷✷✷

ईश्वरार्पितं नेच्छया कृतम् ।
चित्तशोधकं मुक्तिसाधकम् ॥ ३ ॥

Eeshvaraarpitam nechayaa kratam |
chittashodhakam muktisadhakam ||

When there is total acceptance that all actions happen purely by the will of God, and if the fruits and the consequences are accepted as His grace the mind gets purified and attains freedom from expectation.

✷✷✷

कायवाङ्मन कार्यमत्तम् ।
पूजनं जपश्चिन्तनं कमात् ॥ ४ ॥

Kaayavangmanaha karyamuttamam |
poojanam japaschintanam kramaat ||

Accepting and understanding that God has created the world for His sport and God is playing the *lila* through billions of body-mind organisms is better than chanting the sacred names of the Lord which in turn is superior to worshipping the image of the Lord with body, mind and speech.

❧❧❧

जगत ईशधीयुक्तसेवनम् ।
अष्टमूर्तिभृद्देवपूजनम् ॥ ५ ॥

Jagata eeshadhiyuktasevanam |
ashtamoortibruddevapoojanam ||

When there is an understanding that God Himself has become the manifestation; when, by His grace, one feels His presence in the phenomenal existence one obtains the blessing of worshipping the lord of eight-fold forms without neglecting one's responsibilities.

§§§

उत्तमस्तवादुच्चमन्दतः ।
चित्तजं जपध्यानमुत्तमम् ॥ ६ ॥

Uttamastavaadducchmandataha |
chitajam japa dhyaanamuttamam ॥

Understanding that nothing happens according to 'my' will and merely witnessing the billions of body-mind organisms act under God's will is excellent. It is superior to singing the glories of the Lord or reciting His sacred names.

§§§

आज्यधारया स्रोतसा समम् ।
सरलचिन्तनं विरलतः परम् ॥ ७ ॥

Aajyadhaarayaa strotasaa samam |
saralachintanam viralataha param ॥

When there is an understanding that God's will prevails all the time impersonal witnessing happens. It is like the stream of *ghee* (clarified butter) or the flow of a river. This is true meditation. It is much better than meditating with an assumption that one has free will.

❧❧❧

भेदभावनात्सोऽहमित्यसौ ।
भावनाऽभिदा पावनी मता ॥ ८ ॥

Bhedabhaavanaatsohomityasau |
bhavanaabhidaa paavani mataa ॥

The non-dualistic approach of understanding that 'I AM' is God is far more purifying and superior than the dualistic approach of assuming the difference between God and the 'me' and struggling to be one with Him.

❧❧❧

भावशून्यसद्भावसुस्थिति ।
भावनाबलात् भक्तिरुत्तमा ॥ ९ ॥

Bhaavashoonyasadbhaava sustitiha |
bhaavanaabalaat bhaktiruttamaa ||

By the grace of God or the Master when one is
firmly established in the 'I AM', devoid of the
thinking mind, with an impersonal knowing that
there is no 'me' to get involved, that is supreme
Devotion.

❧❧❧

हस्थले मन ः स्वस्थता किया ।
भक्तियोगबोधाश्च निश्चितम् ॥ १० ॥

Hritstale manaha svastataa kriyaa |
bhaktiyogabodhaascha nischitam ||

The dissolving of the thinking mind in the Heart,
purely by the grace of God or the Master, is true
devotion, Yoga and understanding.

❧❧❧

वायुरोधनाल्लीयते मनः ।
जालपक्षिवद्रोधसाधनम् ॥ ११ ॥

Vayurodhanaalleeyate manaha |
jaalapakshivadrodasaadanam ॥

Through the act of regulating breath the mind is
subdued, just as a bird is restrained when caught
in a net. This helps in checking the involvement of
the thinking mind at that moment.

৬৬৬

चित्तवायवश्चित्क्रियायुताः ।
शाखयोर्द्वयी शक्तिमूलका ॥ १२ ॥

Chittavaayavashchit kriyaayutaaha |
shaakhayordvayee shaktimoolakaa ॥

Thought   and   breath   have   their   origins   in
Consciousness

৬৬৬

लयविनाशने उभयरोधने ।
लयगतं पुनर्भवति नो मृतम् ॥१३॥

Layavinaashane ubhayarodone |
layagatam punarbhavati no mritam ॥

When the mind is absorbed, in work or otherwise, and the thinking mind is not active it may be said that the mind is in control temporarily, only to become active again. When through the deep understanding that, 'God is the doer and no "one" has any control over thoughts and actions' the thinking mind is totally annihilated then it can be said that the thinking mind in that body-mind organism is dead and only the working mind remains.

✷✷✷

प्राणवन्धनाल्लीनमानसम् ।
एकचिन्तनान्नाशमेत्यदः ॥१४॥

Praanabhandanaalleenamaanasam |
ekchintanaannaashametyadaha ॥

The thinking mind can be temporarily suspended

through the control of breath. It can be annihilated only when there is total understanding that God's will prevails all the time and the different forms are only puppets having no free will of their own. With this understanding three beautiful things happen: there is no 'one' to feel guilty or proud, to get frustrated or to have a sense of enmity. Life becomes simple.

✺✺✺

नष्टमानसोत्कृष्टयोगिनः ।
कृत्यमस्ति किं स्वस्थितिं यतः ॥ १५ ॥

Nashtamaanasotkrushtayoginaha |
krityamasti kim svastitim yataha ॥

The sage, whose thinking mind has been destroyed by the total acceptance of the fact that nothing happens unless it is the will of God, and who rests in the 'I AM' does all actions with the knowledge that Consciousness alone functions through the billions of body-mind organism.

दृश्यवारितं चित्तमात्मनः ।
चित्त्वदर्शनं तत्त्वदर्शनम् ॥१६॥

Drushyvaaritam chittamaatmanaha |
chitvadarshanam tatvadarshanam ||

With the realization that the 'me' that was all the
time considering itself a separate entity is only a
dreamed character, the mind turns away from
objects and gets focussed on the 'I AM'. That is the
true vision of Reality.

***

मानसं तु किं मार्गणे कृते ।
नैव मानसं मार्ग आर्जवात् ॥१७॥

Maanasam tu kim maargane krite |
naiva maanasam maarge aarjavaat ||

When the enquiry, 'What is the mind?' occurs
there is a direct experience that the mind does not
exist and that thinking is only an appearance in
consciousness. The ego then surrenders to the 'I
Am' and unnecessary thinking ceases. This is the
direct path.

वृत्तयस्त्वहं वृत्तिमाश्रिताः ।
वृत्तयो मनो विध्दयहं मनः ॥१८॥

Vrattayastavaham – vrittimaashritaahaa |
Vrittayo mano vidyaham manaha ॥

In the ordinary man when a thought occurs the
ego takes delivery of it as 'my thought' and gets
involved. The thinking mind is nothing but the ego
identifying with a thought and getting involved.
In the enlightened Sage, when a thought arises,
witnessing happens and involvement with the
thought does not take place. Ramana Maharshi
says, 'The Sage has no thinking mind and therefore
there are no "others" for him.'

❧❧❧

अहमयं कुतो भवति चिन्वतः ।
अयि पतत्यहं निजविचारणम् ॥१९॥

Ahamayam kruto bhavati chinvataha |
Ayee Patatyaham nijavichaaranam ॥

When one enquires, 'Where has the "me" come

from?' it will vanish into Consciousness revealing the truth that the 'me' has really come from Totality as part of the Divine Hypnosis. Consciousness has created the ego and Consciousness will annihilate the ego by initiating the process of self-enquiry.

ᔍᔍᔍ

अहमि नाशभाज्यहमहंतया ।
स्फुरति हृत्स्वयं परमपूर्णसत् ॥२०॥

Ahami naashabhaajyahamahamtaya |
sfurati hratsvayam paramapoornasat ॥

When we accept that God's will prevails all the time, the 'me' as the doer gets smaller and smaller till it gets completely merged in Consciousness.

ᔍᔍᔍ

इदमहंपदाभिख्यमन्वहम् ।
अहमिलीनकेऽप्यलयसत्तया ॥२१॥

Idamahampadaabhikyamanvaham |
ahamileenakepyalaya sattayaa ॥

When the sense of personal doership disappears with the total acceptance that 'All there is, is Consciousness' the thinking mind ceases to exist during the waking hours as in deep sleep. What remains is the light of pure Consciousness, the indestructible 'I AM'.

❧❧❧

विग्रहेन्द्रियप्राणधीतमः ।
नाहमेकसत्तज्जडं ह्यसत् ॥ २२ ॥

Vigrahendriyapraana dheetamaha |
naahamekasattajadam hyasat ॥

Our true nature is God. It is not the body or the senses, or the mind, or breath, or ignorance. These are inert. They totally depend on Consciousness for existence.

❧❧❧

सत्त्वभासिका चित्क्वचेतरा ।
सत्याहिचिच्चित्या ह्यहम् ॥ २३ ॥

Satvabhaasika chitkvavetaraa |
sattayaahichicchitayaa hyaham ॥

Seeking generally begins with the seeker wanting to know God through various means until Totality or the Master makes him understand the error of usurping the pure subjectivity of God and reducing Him into an object. Ramana Maharshi says, 'Only Consciousness knows itself because Consciousness is all there is. The ego cannot know God. It can only merge into Consciousness through understanding and surrender.'

***

ईशजीवयोर्वेषधीभिदा ।
सत्स्वभावतो वस्तु केवलम् ॥ २४ ॥

Eeshajeevayorveshadheebhidaa |
satsvabhaavato vastu kevalam ॥

The Impersonal and the identified Consciousness are essentially the same. The Sage has no ego or the thinking mind and is not attached to any form; the man of ignorance feels that the ego and the form are real and is totally ignorant of the Self.

***

वेषहानतः स्वात्मदर्शनम् ।
ईशदर्शनं स्वात्मरूपतः ॥ २५ ॥

Veshahaanataha svaatmadarshanam |
eeshadarshanam svaatmaroopataha ॥

When the Impersonal Consciousness liberates
the identified Consciousness from the sense of
doership and thereby brings about realization
that the Source is all there is, it can be said that
the individual had a vision of the Lord as the Self.

❧❧❧

आत्मसंस्थितिः स्वात्मदर्शनम् ।
आत्मनिर्द्वयादात्मदिष्ठता ॥ २६ ॥

Aatmasamstitiha svaatmadarshanam |
aatmanirdvayaadaatmanishtathaa ॥

When the doership of the ego is totally annihilated
the vision of the Self occurs. There is an impersonal
knowing that the Self is all and the firm abidance
in the Self happens.

ज्ञानवर्जिताऽज्ञानहीनचित् ।

ज्ञानमस्ति किं ज्ञातुमन्तरम् ॥ २७ ॥

jnaanavarjitaa jnaanaheenachit |
jnaanamasti kim jnaatumantaram ॥

True knowing is the understanding that Consciousness functions through all the living beings. This Knowledge is beyond the intellectual 'knowledge' or 'ignorance'. After enlightenment, when there is clear understanding that only Consciousness acts what else is there to be known?

✿✿✿

किं स्वरूपमित्यात्मदर्शने ।
अव्ययाभवापूर्णचित्सुखम् ॥ २८ ॥

Kim swaroopamityaatma darshane |
avyayaabhavaa poornachitsukham ॥

When one enquires, 'What is my true nature?' one begins to realize that one's true nature is beyond birth, death and decay. It is God or Consciousness.

✿✿✿

वन्धमुक्त्यतीतं परं सुखम् ।
विन्दतीह जीवस्तु दैविकः ॥२९॥

Bandhamuktyateetam param sukham |
vindateeha jeevastu daivikaha ||

When the 'me' understands and accepts that it is
God who functions through all the living beings
it goes beyond the thoughts of freedom and
bondage.

❈❈❈

अहमपेतकं निजविभानकम् ।
महदिदंतपो रमणवागियम् ॥३०॥

Ahamapetakam nijavibhaanakam |
mahadidamtapo Ramanavaagiyam ||

When the 'me' disappears in terms of doership
and it is realized that 'Consciousness is all there
is', it is excellent *tapas*, Ramana says this.

❈❈❈

Noumenal Living

✱✱✱

Ramana Maharshi says, 'Watch the breath.' Breath becomes quicker when the mind is agitated. As you watch the breath the mind becomes quieter. Watch your breath as passively as you can. The idea is to keep the thought out. A thought leads to horizontal thinking. If your brain is busy witnessing the breath then a thought cannot come from outside.

Watching one's breath is only in the beginning. Ultimately the mind which is watching the breath has to disappear.

Meditation for me means 'no thinking mind'. Absence of thinking is the presence of Impersonal Awareness. The state away from unnecessary thinking is the only real state.

Confusion arises when you don't like what is happening. An event happens by the will of God. You think it was 'your' will and get confused.

Merely witness whatever is happening.

A thought comes, watch it go. Another thought comes, watch it go. The sage does not react to the biological reaction. The ordinary man reacts to the biological reaction in the body-mind organism but does not react to the actual thing.

True meditation is accepting whatever happens as God's will.

The understanding that 'nobody can ever be the doer' does not have a solution to your problems. This understanding will bring about an *attitude* which will make it easier for you find to a solution.

'What do I do until the final understanding happens?'

Ramesh says, 'Very simple. You act *as if* the final understanding has happened.'

Tukaram the Bhakta says,

> *'I went to see God,*
> *I came back being God.'*

✷✷✷

Abhangas
AND THEIR MEANING

❧❧❧

Gurur Bramha, Gurur Vishnu /
Gurur Devo Maheshwara //
Gurur Saakshaath Parabramha /
Tasmai Shri Guruvenamaha //

My Guru is Lord Brahma, Lord Vishnu, and Lord
Maheshwara (Lord Shiva). My Guru is the Supreme
Self Incarnate. I salute my Guru who is God Incarnate.

1

Namo Aadiroopaa Omkaara Swaroopaa /
Viswaachiya Roopaa Maayabaapaa //
Tuziyaa Saattene Tuze Guna Gaavoo /
Tene Sukhi Raahu Sarvakaala //
Toochi Shrotaa Toochi Vaktaa
Jnaanaasi Anjana /
Sarva Hone Jaane Tuzyaa Haati //
Tukaa Mhane Yethe Naahi Mee Too Pana /
Stavaave Te Kavana Kavanaalaagi //
Namo Aadiroopaa Omkaara Swaroopaa /
Viswaachiya Roopaa Maayabaapaa //

My salutations to You, who are beyond all forms. My
salutations to You, who are the core of my Being. My
salutations to the all-pervading Consciousness which is
the source of the entire manisfestation. By your grace I
will sing hymns praising You and remain happy all the
time, enjoying the pleasure and suffering the pain in the
moment. I am totally convinced that both the talking
and the listening happen by Your will. Nothing can
happen unless it is Your will. Tukaram says, 'There is
no sense of being separate from You. Whom do I praise,
for what?'

2

Omkaara Swaroopaa Sadguru Samarthaa /
Omkaara Swaroopaa Sadguru Samarthaa /
Anaathaanchyaa Naathaa Tuja Namo /
Tuja Namo / Tuja Namo / Tuja Namo / Tuja Namo //
Omkaara Swaroopaa Sadguru Samarthaa /
Anaathaanchyaa Naathaa Tuja Namo /
Tuja Namo / Tuja Namo / Tuja Namo / Tuja Namo //
Namo Maayabaapaa / Gurukripaa ghanaa /
Todiyaa Bandhanaa Maayaa Mohaa /
Namo Maayabaapaa I Gurukripaa ghanaa /
Todiyaa Bandhanaa Maayaa Mohaa /
Moha Jaala Maaze Kona Nirasheela /
Tuzaveena Dayaalaa Sadgururaaya /
Tuzaveena Dayaalaa Sadgururaaya //
Tuja Namo I Tuja Namo I Tuja Namo //
Omkaara Swaroopaa Sadguru Samarthaa /
Anaathaanchyaa Naathaa Tuja Namo /
Tuja Namo /Tuja Namo / Tuja Namo / Tuja Namo //
Sadgururaayaa Maazaa Anandasagar /
Trilokya Aadhaar Gururaav /
Trilokya Aadhaar Gururaav /
Trilokya Aadhaar Gururaav /

Gururaaj Swaami Ase Swayam Prakaash /
Jyaa Pudhe Udaasa Chandra Ravi /
Jyaa Pudhe Udaasa Chandra Ravi /
Jyaa Pudhe Udaasa Chandra Ravi //
Ravi, Shashi, Agni Nenathi Jyaa Roopaa /
Swaprkaasha Roopaa Nene Vedaa /
Swaprkaasha Roopaa Nene Vedaa /
Swaprkaasha Roopaa / Tuja Namo / Tuja Namo //
Omkaara Swaroopaa Sadguru Samartha /
Anaathaanchyaa Naathaa Tuja Namo /
Tuja Namo / Tuja Namo / Tuja Namo / Tuja Namo //
Ekaa Janardhani Guruparabrahma /
Ekaa Janardhani Guruparabrahma /
Tayaache Pai Naam Sada Mukhi /
Tayaache Pai Naam Sada Mukhi /
Tayaache Pai Naam Sada Mukhi /
Omkaara Swaroopaa Sadguru Samartha /
Anaathaanchyaa Naathaa Tuja Namo /
Tuja Namo / Tuja Namo / Tuja Namo / Tuja Namo //
Tuja Namo / Tuja Namo / Tuja Namo //

Salutations to my dear Sadguru, who has unvanquishable understanding, who is the essence of universal presence and who never forsakes the seeker who comes to Him. You, my divine Father, are a storehouse of Grace itself.

You are primarily responsible for making me realize that I am unnecessarily involved. When will you shower total understanding on this object? I have yet to meet someone more compassionate than you. You are the source of peace for me. Your are my home. All the three worlds owe their existence to the light which shines through you. My beloved Lord Shri Guru is a light to Himself. The I Am shines in all its brilliance through Him. The light of the sun, the moon and fire looks pale compared to Him. The sun, moon and fire do not shine on their own. The Vedas themselves do not have the Light of Understanding. Eka Janardan has found the Self in his Guru. He is extremely happy to contemplate on the words of His Guru with deep gratitude.

❧❧❧

3

Tuja Saguna Mhano Ki Nirguna Re /
Tuja Saguna Mhano Ki Nirguna Re //
Saguna Nirguna Eku Govindu Re /
Eku Govindu Re //
Tuja Saguna Mhano Ki Nirguna Re /
Tuja Saguna Mhano Ki Nirguna Re //
Anumaanenaa, Anumaanena / Shruti
Neti Neti Mhanati Govindu Re / Shruti
Neti Neti Mhanati Govindu Re /
Tuja Saguna Mhano Ki Nirguna Re /
Tuja Saguna Mhano Ki Nirguna Re /
Tuja Drishya Mhano Ki Adrishya Re /
Tuja Drishya Mhano Ki Adrishya Re /
Drishya Adrishya Eku Govindu Re /
Drishya Adrishya Eku Govindu Re //
Tuja Saguna Mhano Ki Nirguna Re /
Tuja Saguna Mhano Ki Nirguna Re //
Tuja Aaakaaru Mhano Ki
Niraakaaru Re /
Tuja Aaakaaru Mhano Ki
Niraakaaru Re //
Aakaaru Niraakaaru Eku Govindu Re /

Aakaaru Niraakaaru Eku Govindu Re //
Tuja Saguna Mhano Ki Nirguna Re /
Tuja Saguna Mhano Ki Nirguna Re //
Tuja Sthoola Mhano Ki Sookshma Re /
Tuja Sthoola Mhano Ki Sookshma Re //
Sthoola Sookshma Eku Govindu Re /
Sthoola Sookshma Eku Govindu Re //
Tuja Saguna Mhano Ki Nirguna Re /
Tuja Saguna Mhano Ki Nirguna Re //
Nivritti Prasade Jnanadeva Bole /
Jnaanadeva Bole /
Baaparakumadevivaru Viththalu Re /
Nivritti Prasade Jnanadeva Bole /
Baaparakumadevivaru Viththalu Re /
Tuja Saguna Mhano Ki Nirguna Re /
Tuja Saguna Mhano Ki Nirguna Re //
Saguna Nirguna Eku Govindu Re /
Eku Govindu Re //
Tuja Saguna Mhano Ki Nirguna Re /
Tuja Saguna Mhano Ki Nirguna Re //

Govinda! (Lord Krishna) can I praise You by giving You attributes or are You beyond all attributes? I have realised, by my Guru's grace, that you have attributes and you also exist without any attribute. Do not doubt these words, my friends. The shruti says, 'Not this, not that' and arrives at the I Am, the impersonal Awareness of Being, the One who is my Govinda. Are You the gross or the subtle Govinda? In phenomenality Govinda is all there is – gross and subtle. Are You with form or without, Govinda? You alone are, in all the forms and beyond. Do I call You manifest or unmanifest, Govinda? You are the source of all manifestation. The Source alone is. By the grace and authorization from my Guru Nivritti, Jnanadev says, 'All there is, is Vitthala (Lord Krishna).'

❧❧❧

4

Hechi Daana Degaa Devaa /
Tuzaa Visara Na Vhaavaa /
Visara Na Vhaavaa /
Tuzaa Visara Na Vhaavaa //
Hechi Daana Degaa Devaa /
Tuzaa Visara Na Vhaavaa /
Visara Na Vhaavaa /
Tuzaa Visara Na Vhaavaa //
Guna Gaayeen Aavadi Hechi Maazi
Sarva Jodi /
Maazi Sarva Jodi /
Hechi Maazi Sarva Jodi //
Nala Ge Mukti Dhana Sampada /
Nala Ge Mukti Dhana Sampada //
Santa Sanga Dei Sadaa /
Santa Sanga Dei Sadaa /
Santa Sanga Dei Sadaa //
Tukaa Mhane Tukaa Mhane Garbhavaasi Sukhe
Ghaalaave Aamhasi /
Sukhe Ghaalaave Aamhasi /
Sukhe Ghaalaave Aamhasi //
Guna Gayeen Aavadi Hechi Maazi

Sarva Jodi /
Maazi Sarva Jodi /
Hechi Maazi Sarva Jodi //
Hechi Daana Degaa Devaa /
Tuzaa Visara Na Vhaavaa /
Visara Na Vhaavaa /
Tuzaa Visara Na Vhaavaa //
Hechi Daana Degaa Devaa /
Tuzaa Visara Na Vhaavaa /
Visara Na Vhaavaa /
Tuzaa Visara Na Vhaavaa //

Give me only one boon, my Lord: May I never forget that Your will alone prevails. I will joyfully sing of Your glorious deeds. Give me the association of people who have total trust in You. I don't care for Liberation, fame, or fortune. Tukaram says, 'If you don't want Enlightenment to happen in this body, let it not happen. Give me as many births as you want my Lord – I don't care.'

✿✿✿

5

Tuze Roopa Chitti Raaho /
Mukhi Tuze Naama /
Tuze Roopa Chitti Raaho /
Mukhi Tuze Naama /
Deha Prapanchaachaa Daasa /
Sukhe Karo Kaama /
Sukhe Karo Kaama //
Tuze Roopa Chitti Raaho /
Mukhi Tuze Naama /
Dehadhaari Jo Jo Tyaache Vihita Nitya Karma /
Sadaachaara Sanmaargaachaa /
Aagalaa Na Dharma /
Dehadhaari Jo Jo Tyaache Vihita Nitya Karma /
Sadaachaara Sanmaargaachaa /
Aagalaa Na Dharma //
Tulaa Aavade Te Haati /
Ghade Nitya Karma /
Tulaa Aavade Te Haati /
Ghade Nitya Karma /
Deha Prapanchaachaa Daasa /
Sukhe Karo Kaama /
Sukhe Karo Kaama //

Tuze Roopa Chitti Raho /
Mukhi Tuze Naama /
Tujhya Padi Vaahilaa Mee /
Dehabhaava Saaraa /
Ude Antaraali Aatmaa /
Soduni Pasaara /
Tujhya Padi Vaahilaa Mee /
Dehabhaava Saaraa /
Ude Antaraali Aatmaa /
Soduni Pasaara /
Naam Tuze Gheto Goraa /
Naam Tuze Gheto Goraa /
Houni Nishkaama //
Naam Tuze Gheto Goraa /
Houni Nishkama //
Deha Prapanchaachaa Daasa /
Sukhe Karo Kaama /
Sukhe Karo Kaama //
Tuze Roopa Chitti Raho /
Mukhi Tuze Naama /
Tuze Roopa Chitti Raho /
Mukhi Tuze Naama //
Panduranga Panduranga

May Your form be in my heart and Your name on my lips. The body is subject to the laws of phenomenality. Let it do the work assigned to it by God. Body-mind organisms react strictly according to the way they are programmed. I truly understand that there is no good path or good conduct for the instrument other than the way it is programmed (genes and up to date conditioning). Only those actions which You want, and for which You have uniquely programmed this body-mind organism happen all the time. Having understood this, I can only surrender at Your feet. May the 'I Am' in this body soar into the sky and not get involved with phenomenality. Gora recites Your name with great feeling and without any expectation.

Translated by Shirishkumar S. Murthy
by the grace of his Master, Ramesh S. Balsekar

❧❧❧